Seafood Simple

Simple, Delicious Seafood Recipes for
Hectic Nights and Relaxing Weekends

Authors:
Sarah M. Godbold
&
Scott S. Jones

Illustrator:
Paul M. Mason

Published by Atlantic Products, LLC
Boston, Massachusetts

Text © 2005 by Atlantic Products, LLC
Cover Art and Illustrations © Paul M. Mason

Printed in the United States of America

10 9 8 7 6 5 4 3 2

Table *of*
Contents

Introduction

Americans have a love affair with seafood. In fact, consumption of seafood in the U.S. has increased dramatically since the early 1980s. Yet for many people seafood remains exotic – something to be ordered at a restaurant or enjoyed at the home of a "gourmet" friend or family member. Even people who cook seafood for themselves often feel limited to a few basic recipes.

The secret, however, is that delicious seafood is actually simple to purchase and prepare. In terms of buying, it is no longer necessary to live near the docks or even a "specialty" seafood market. Top quality seafood is now readily available in wholesale clubs and supermarkets at terrific prices – often less expensive than chicken or beef.

As for preparation, there are many different cooking options that are simple, quick and delicious. In fact, seafood is so simple to prepare, the trickiest part is not overcooking it. With its naturally tender flesh, seafood absorbs seasonings well. So the difference between a memorable seafood event and one you'd rather forget often comes down to overcooking.

Of course, seafood is also an extremely healthful choice – a source of lean protein, with virtually no saturated fats or carbs, yet rich in B-complex vitamins and oils that actually lower "bad" (LDL) cholesterol.

As our title suggests, our purpose is to share the secret of simple seafood, with concise species and nutritional information, easy buying and prepping instructions and simple, delicious recipes for both hectic weeknights and hopefully more relaxing weekends – all conveniently divided among popular and commonly available species.

So enjoy and pass along the secret to your friends and family – seafood is simple!

3 easy tips *to* avoid overcooking *seafood...*

The 10-Minute Rule

This is an easy rule to remember cooking times for baked fish. In a 400°F oven, let fish bake for 10 minutes for every 1 inch of thickness. So, for a 1 1/2" thick salmon fillet, bake in a 400°F oven for about 15 minutes.

The Fork Test

This is an easy test to determine when your fish is done cooking. Simply insert a regular fork into the thickest part of the fillet, then withdraw and feel the tines. If the tines are warm to the touch, the fish should be finished cooking. If the tines are cold, the fish is not done.

The Flake Test

Fish should flake easily when it's through cooking. To test this, gently cut away a tiny edge of your fish with a fork. If there is little (or no) resistance when you separate the meat with the fork, it is done.

Salmon

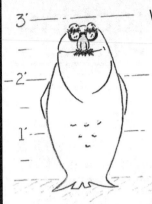

We are fortunate today to have large quantities of salmon available year round, both farm raised and wild.

No other species of fish is more versatile than salmon. It can easily be baked, broiled, poached or grilled. It also marinates beautifully and easily.

Salmon comes in a number of species, but the most commonly available in the U.S. is Atlantic salmon, which is farm raised in North America, South America and Europe. Atlantic salmon has silver skin with black dots, and the whole fish is typically 4 – 18 pounds in size. Atlantic salmon has a delicious flavor with firm, pale-orange meat.

Although much has been made of farm-raised salmon lately in the press, it is perfectly safe and healthful to eat with lower concentrations of chemicals (such as PCBs) than chicken or beef and less fat than wild salmon.

Salmon is also one of the best sources of "omega-3" essential fatty acids (with about 1.4 grams per 100 grams of salmon). Omega-3s cannot be made by the body and therefore must be included in your diet. They play a crucial role in nerve tissue, healthy eyes and in the prevention of heart disease. Research has also found that low omega-3 levels are related to depression and other mood disorders. Not surprisingly, modern western diets are severely deficient in omega-3s.

Salmon

Like all of the seafood described in this book, salmon can be purchased at your local supermarket or wholesale club, and fresh fillets should be used within two to three days of purchase. Simply keep them wrapped in your refrigerator. Unlike many types of fish (which will begin to "cook" in a marinade after only 30 minutes), salmon can be marinated for up to six hours.

Salmon typically comes filleted with either the skin on or off. It does not matter whether you purchase salmon with or without skin. The following recipes assume that the salmon is skinless. If you use salmon with the skin on, simply remove the skin prior to preparation or as the last step in each recipe before serving.

Remember to rinse salmon (and all other fish) fillets in cold water and then pat dry with paper towels prior to cooking.

Nutritional Information

Atlantic Salmon	*Serving size: 100g/3.5oz raw*
Calories	183
Fat Calories	97.2
Total Fat	10.8g
Saturated Fat	2.2g
Carbohydrates	0.0g
Cholesterol	59.0mg
Sodium	59.0mg
Protein	19.9g
Omega-3	1.4g

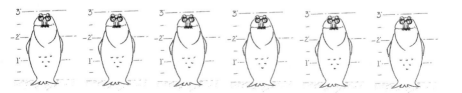

Salmon

Weeknight Recipes   *(Each Serves 4)*

BAKED SALMON IN GARLIC SAUCE

1 1/2 – 2 pound salmon fillet, cut into 4 pieces
2 garlic cloves, peeled and chopped
1/4 teaspoon salt
1/4 teaspoon pepper
3 tablespoons unsalted butter
1 tablespoon fresh lemon juice
1/4 cup minced parsley
Lemon wedges

- Preheat oven to 400°F.
- Mash up garlic pieces in the salt and pepper with a fork.
- Mix butter into the garlic paste.
- Put salmon in a single layer on a baking tray.
- Top salmon with garlic paste and squeeze lemon juice on top.
- Bake for 10 – 15 minutes until salmon is cooked through.
- Serve with minced parsley and lemon wedges.

GRILLED SALMON WITH CITRUS GLAZE

1 1/2 – 2 pound salmon fillet, cut into 4 pieces
Olive oil
Salt and pepper to taste

- Brush salmon with olive oil.
- Place salmon on a moderately hot grill, top side down.
- Grill salmon for 3 – 5 minutes per side, until both sides are just cooked through.
- Remove from grill and drizzle with citrus glaze before serving.

Salmon

CITRUS GLAZE

> 1/2 cup balsamic vinegar (do not substitute)
> 1/2 cup dry white wine
> 2 tablespoons fresh lemon juice
> 2 tablespoons brown sugar
> Pepper to taste

- Bring all ingredients to a boil in a small saucepan.
- Cook over moderately high heat for 3 – 4 minutes until mixture thickens.
- Let cool slightly before drizzling over grilled salmon.

Tip: This glaze makes up well and stores in the refrigerator for up to 3 weeks! Just remember to warm slightly before using. This glaze tastes great on other grilled meats as well.

BAKED SALMON DIJON

> 1 1/2 – 2 pound salmon fillet, cut into 4 pieces
> 1/2 cup sweet onion, thinly sliced
> 1/2 cup mayonnaise (reduced fat may be used)
> 2 tablespoons Dijon mustard
> 2 teaspoons fresh lemon juice
> Pepper to taste

- Preheat oven to 375°F.
- In a small bowl, mix mayo, mustard and lemon juice.
- Season salmon with pepper.
- Place a few slices of onion on each salmon piece.
- Cover salmon evenly with the mayo mixture.
- Put salmon in a single layer in an ovenproof pan.
- Bake for 20 – 25 minutes. (Topping should be lightly browned and salmon cooked through.)

Salmon

GRILLED TERIYAKI SALMON

> 1 1/2 – 2 pound salmon fillet, cut into 4 pieces
> 3 tablespoons soy sauce
> 2 tablespoons fresh lemon or lime juice
> 2 tablespoons vegetable oil
> 1 clove garlic, minced and crushed
> 1/2 teaspoon sugar
> 1/2 teaspoon pepper
> 1 tablespoon honey

- In a large, resealable plastic bag, mix together all ingredients except salmon.
- Put salmon in bag and press well to coat thoroughly.
- Refrigerate salmon in bag for at least 30 minutes (and no more than 2 hours).
- Place marinated salmon on a moderately hot grill, top side down.
- Grill salmon for 3 – 5 minutes per side, until both sides are just cooked through.

Tip: A great shortcut for this dish is to buy a quality teriyaki sauce and "doctor it up" with a little fresh lemon juice. The bottled teriyaki sauces tend to be a bit strong.

FRIED PEPPERED SALMON

> 1 1/2 – 2 pound salmon fillet, cut into 4 pieces
> 3 tablespoons soy sauce
> 1 teaspoon sugar
> 2 tablespoons pepper
> 1/2 teaspoon salt
> 1 – 2 tablespoons vegetable oil

- Mix soy sauce and sugar in a resealable plastic bag.
- Add salmon to soy mixture, coating salmon thoroughly.

Salmon

- Refrigerate salmon in bag for at least 1 hour (up to 6 hours).
- Remove salmon from marinade and pat dry with a paper towel.
- Coat salmon on all sides with pepper.
- Sprinkle salmon with salt.
- In a nonstick skillet, heat oil until moderately hot.
- Place marinated salmon top side down in skillet and fry for 5 minutes.
- Turn salmon over and reduce heat to medium.
- Fry salmon for another 5 minutes until just cooked through.

Weekend Recipes   *(Each Serves 4)*

EASY POACHED SALMON WITH TARRAGON SAUCE

1 1/2 – 2 pound salmon fillet, cut into 4 pieces
2 1/2 cups white wine (or fish broth or clam juice may be substituted)
2 1/2 cups water
Salt and pepper to taste

- Bring wine (or fish broth or clam juice) and water to a simmer in a large skillet.
- Add salmon.
- Low simmer for 8 minutes. (If needed, add enough hot water to cover fillets.)
- Add salt and pepper to taste.
- Remove salmon with a slotted spoon.
- Spoon tarragon sauce over salmon immediately before serving.

Tip: Fish may be poached one day ahead and kept chilled. Bring to room temperature before serving.

Salmon

TARRAGON SAUCE

2 bunches fresh tarragon
1 bunch fresh chives
1 shallot
3/4 cup flat leaf parsley, chopped
1 cup mayonnaise
1/3 cup rice wine vinegar
2 teaspoons Dijon mustard
Salt and pepper to taste

- Pick tarragon leaves to measure 1/2 cup.
- Chop chives to measure 1/3 cup.
- Coarsely chop shallot.
- Put tarragon, chives and shallot into a food processor.
- Puree, adding remaining ingredients until smooth.
- Spoon over cooked salmon when ready to serve.

Tip: Also can be prepared one day ahead. Bring to room temperature before serving.

GRILLED SALMON WITH COCONUT SAUCE

1 1/2 – 2 pound salmon fillet, cut into 4 pieces
1 cup canned unsweetened coconut milk
Zest of 1 lime (see note below)
1 anchovy fillet (or 1 teaspoon of anchovy paste
may be substituted)
1 fresh, seeded jalapeno
1/2 cup fresh basil leaves
1/2 cup fresh cilantro leaves
Sea salt

- Place coconut milk, lime zest, anchovy fillet (or paste), jalapeno, basil and cilantro in a food processor or blender.
- Process coconut milk mixture until smooth.
- Place salmon in a shallow dish and pour coconut sauce over.

Salmon

- Marinate salmon in the covered dish in refrigerator for at least 30 minutes (up to 8 hours).
- Remove salmon from sauce, brushing off excess sauce.
- Place remaining sauce in a small saucepan.
- Sprinkle salmon lightly with salt.
- Place salmon on moderately hot grill, top side down.
- Grill salmon for 3 – 5 minutes per side, until both sides are just cooked through.
- While salmon is grilling, bring sauce to a boil and then simmer for 5 minutes.
- Spoon sauce over cooked salmon and serve immediately.

Note: "Zest" is simply the outer layer of a fruit's skin. In the case of a lime, it's the green (but not white) part of its skin. To get the zest, simply remove the green layer of the lime's skin with a vegetable peeler or a grater.

PAN-SEARED, DRY-RUBBED SALMON WITH TOMATO BASIL SAUCE

1 1/2 – 2 pound salmon fillet, cut into 4 pieces
1 tablespoon olive oil
Dry rub:
2 tablespoons pepper
2 tablespoons dried thyme
2 tablespoons Adobo seasoning (see note below)
2 tablespoons paprika
4 tablespoons flour
2 teaspoons cayenne pepper

- Combine dry rub spices.
- Rub into both sides of salmon pieces, pressing in well.
- In a large skillet, heat olive oil over medium heat.
- Place salmon in skillet top side down for 3 minutes, until a nice crust is formed.
- Turn salmon over and cook for another 4 – 5 minutes until just cooked through.

Salmon

- Spoon tomato basil sauce over salmon and serve immediately.

Note: Adobo spice is found in the Mexican (or Hispanic/Latin) section of your market. If you cannot find it, mix together 2 teaspoons pepper, 1 teaspoon cayenne pepper, 1 teaspoon cumin, 1/2 teaspoon garlic powder and 1/2 teaspoon onion powder.

TOMATO BASIL SAUCE

> 2 teaspoons olive oil
> 2 tablespoons cherry tomatoes, halved
> 2 tablespoons dry vermouth
> 2/3 cup heavy cream
> Dash of cayenne pepper
> Salt to taste
> 8 basil leaves, cut in a chiffonade (see note below)

- Heat olive oil in a large saucepan over medium-high heat.
- Add halved tomatoes and sauté for 3 minutes, tossing often. (Tomatoes should begin to soften and brown slightly.)
- Add vermouth, reducing heat to low.
- Add heavy cream and cayenne pepper.
- Cook for 2 minutes or until sauce has thickened.
- Season with salt to taste and 1/2 of the basil.
- Remove sauce from heat and spoon over cooked salmon.
- Garnish with remaining basil.

Note: To cut in a chiffonade, stack the basil leaves one on top of the other and roll tightly into a cylinder. Then slice the cylinder of leaves crosswise into thin strips.

Tip: For an extra special evening, add 1/2 cup cooked lobster or crabmeat to tomato basil sauce before serving!

Salmon

PEPPERED SALMON WITH PINEAPPLE SAUCE

1 1/2 – 2 pound salmon fillet, cut into 4 pieces
2 teaspoons olive oil
Salt and pepper to taste

- Brush salmon lightly with olive oil.
- Sprinkle salmon with salt and pepper.
- Place salmon on a moderately hot grill, top side down.
- Grill salmon for 3 – 5 minutes per side, until both sides are just cooked through.
- Serve the salmon with chilled pineapple sauce on the side.

PINEAPPLE SAUCE

2 tablespoons unsalted butter
2 cups fresh pineapple, in chunks
2 tablespoons honey
1/2 of a chipotle chile, canned
3/4 cup orange juice
4 fresh mint leaves

- Sauté pineapple chunks in 1 tablespoon butter in sauté pan for 1 minute.
- Stir in honey and chipotle chile.
- Continue cooking until pineapple has caramelized, about 4 minutes.
- Reduce heat to low and add orange juice.
- Simmer until orange juice is reduced by three quarters.
- Place mixture in a blender or food processor.
- Add mint and puree until smooth.
- Place mixture in a covered bowl and refrigerate before serving.

Salmon

SALMON WITH ANCHOVY-CAPER BUTTER

1 1/2 – 2 pound salmon fillet, cut into 4 pieces
2 teaspoons olive oil
Salt and pepper to taste
3 garlic cloves
2 anchovy fillets (or 2 teaspoons of anchovy
    paste may be substituted)
2 tablespoons capers, drained
1 tablespoon fresh lemon juice
1 tablespoon cognac
1 tablespoon parsley, chopped
1/2 teaspoon pepper
1 stick unsalted butter, room temperature

- Place garlic, anchovies, capers, lemon juice, cognac, parsley and pepper in a food processor.
- Add butter and process until smooth.
- Transfer butter mixture to a piece of plastic wrap and roll into a log.
- Freeze until firm, about 1 hour.
- Brush salmon lightly with olive oil, and sprinkle with salt and pepper.
- Place salmon on a moderately hot grill, top side down.
- Grill salmon for 3 – 5 minutes per side, until both sides are just cooked through.
- Top each piece with a 1/2" slice of the anchovy-caper butter.

Note: As an alternative to grilling, place salmon in a broiler pan on oven rack about 6 inches from the heat. Broil for 8 minutes or until cooked through.

Tip: Anchovy-caper butter may be prepared up to a week ahead and kept frozen. Let butter soften slightly before cutting.

Salmon

ROSEMARY-SCENTED SALMON ON A PLANK

---

1 1/2 – 2 pound salmon fillet, cut in half crosswise
2/3 cup fresh lime juice
2 1/2 tablespoons fresh rosemary, minced
2 tablespoons olive oil
1 teaspoon prepared horseradish
1/2 teaspoon salt
1 teaspoon pepper
1 cedar plank (see note below)

- Soak plank in water for at least 30 minutes.
- In a resealable, plastic bag, mix lime juice, rosemary, oil and horseradish.
- Place salmon in bag, coat thoroughly and refrigerate for 2 hours.
- Remove salmon from marinade and sprinkle with salt and pepper.
- Place cedar plank on grill and heat to medium.
- Place salmon on plank.
- Close grill cover and cook about 20 – 25 minutes until just cooked through.
- Remove salmon from plank, cut each half into 2 pieces and serve.

Note: Cedar planks are available at most cook stores and some supermarkets. Using a plank creates a very moist, delicious salmon!

Salmon

SALMON WITH MUSTARD MAPLE SAUCE

1 1/2 – 2 pound salmon fillet, cut into 4 pieces
Salt and pepper to taste
1 tablespoon vegetable oil

- Lightly season salmon with salt and pepper.
- Heat oil in large skillet to medium-high heat.
- Place salmon in skillet top side down for 4 minutes.
- Turn salmon over and sauté for another 4 minutes until just cooked through.
- Remove to a platter and cover with foil to keep warm.
- Cool skillet slightly and then use to heat through the mustard maple sauce.
- Spoon sauce over salmon and serve immediately.

MUSTARD MAPLE SAUCE

3 tablespoons water
2 tablespoons pure maple syrup
2 tablespoons Dijon mustard
2 garlic cloves, minced
2 teaspoons mustard seeds
1/4 cup green onions, chopped

- Whisk together all ingredients.
- Heat in skillet and spoon over salmon (as described above).

Shrimp

Shrimp is available in so many varieties from all over the world – both farm raised and wild – that it is almost pointless to try to judge shrimp by its color or species. In most cases, you should simply buy shrimp according to the size that you need – small, medium, large or jumbo. (In the seafood business, shrimp are classified by the number of shrimp per pound. So "16-20s" mean that there are 16 to 20 of such shrimp in a pound. Accordingly, "16-20s" generally are considered jumbo shrimp, while "21-25s" are large shrimp.)

Frozen shrimp retains virtually all of its freshness and flavor, and it is great to buy. Because fresh shrimp deteriorates so rapidly, it is almost impossible to find shrimp that has not previously been frozen (unless you happen to live by shrimp docks). In fact, most shrimp is frozen on the boats while they are at sea.

Shrimp is also a highly nutritional food, typically very low in fat and sodium with lots of high quality protein and omega-3 essential fatty acids (like salmon). As you will see, shrimp is incredibly easy to prepare and cooks very quickly, so do not overcook it – overcooked shrimp completely loses its delicious flavor and texture.

As mentioned above, you generally should buy frozen shrimp simply based upon the size that you need, and of course either raw or cooked, depending upon the recipe.

Shrimp

Store shrimp in your freezer and thaw in your refrigerator the night before you plan to serve it (if quicker thawing is absolutely necessary, put shrimp in a strainer and place under cold running water). If the shrimp has already been peeled and deveined by the shrimp company ("P&D" shrimp), then it is ready to be used. If the shrimp is "E-Z peel," then you simply need to remove the pre-split shell with your fingers (the vein has already been removed). If the shrimp is not P&D or E-Z Peel, there is an invaluable tool for peeling and deveining called a shrimp deveiner. It is very inexpensive and available in most cook stores and many supermarkets.

While the shrimp is still partly frozen, insert the tip of the deveiner into the top side of the shrimp's body. Then push the deveiner in toward the tail. As you continue pushing the tip of the tool past the tail, the thicker end of the tool will easily separate the meat from the shell. As the shell separates, gently pull it away. Then use the tip of the tool to remove the black vein (if any) running along the shrimp. Rinse the shrimp under cool running water and drain well.

Nutritional Information

Shrimp	Serving size: 100g/3.5oz raw
Calories	90
Fat Calories	7
Total Fat	0.8g
Saturated Fat	0.2g
Carbohydrates	0.2g
Cholesterol	96.0mg
Sodium	N/A
Protein	19.4g
Omega-3	0.3g

Shrimp

Weeknight Recipes   *(Each Serves 4)*

BOILED SHRIMP

> 2 – 2 1/2 pounds shrimp (medium, large or
>   jumbo), shells on

- In a large pot, bring 3" of cold water to a boil.
- Add shrimp and then cover pot over high heat, stirring occasionally.
- Approximate cooking times:
  - 3 minutes for medium shrimp
  - 5 minutes for large shrimp
  - 6 minutes for jumbo shrimp
- Shrimp are done when they have curled and turned pink.
- Rinse under cold water to stop cooking.
- Peel and eat!

Tip: Cooked shrimp store much better than thawed shrimp. Shrimp should be cooked as soon as possible after thawing (1 day maximum). Once cooked they can be kept covered and refrigerated for 2 days.

SHRIMP COCKTAIL

> 2 pounds large boiled shrimp (see Boiled
>   Shrimp recipe above)
> 1/2 cup bottled seafood sauce
> Lemon wedges

- After boiled shrimp has cooled, peel (leaving tail shell on).
- Serve well-chilled shrimp cocktail on crushed ice, using a good bottled seafood sauce.
- Tuck fresh lemon wedges throughout.

Shrimp

SPICY PEEL AND EAT SHRIMP

> 2 1/2 pounds medium shrimp, shells on
> 1/4 cup Old Bay seasoning
> Lemon wedges
> 1 can of beer

- In a large pot, bring beer and 2" of water to a boil.
- Add shrimp and sprinkle on Old Bay seasoning.
- Cover and steam for 5 minutes, until firm and cooked through.
- Serve shrimp unpeeled with lemon wedges and extra Old Bay seasoning for dipping.

BAKED SHRIMP

> 2 1/2 pounds medium shrimp, peeled and deveined
> Salt and pepper to taste
> 1/2 cup fresh lemon juice
> 1 cup butter, melted
> 1/2 teaspoon oregano
> 2 bay leaves, crushed

- Preheat oven to 375°F.
- In a casserole dish place a layer of shrimp, then sprinkle with salt and pepper.
- Continue layering shrimp with salt and pepper.
- Mix lemon juice, butter, oregano and bay leaves.
- Pour mixture over layered shrimp.
- Bake uncovered for 25 minutes, until shrimp is pink, stirring occasionally.

Tip: Juices from cooked shrimp taste great basted on toasted French bread.

Shrimp

GRILLED GARLIC SHRIMP

> 2 pounds large (or jumbo) shrimp, peeled
>   and deveined
> 12 whole cloves garlic, peeled
> 1/3 cup olive oil
> 1/4 cup tomato sauce
> 2 tablespoons red wine vinegar
> 1 1/2 teaspoons basil
> 1/2 teaspoon salt
> 1/2 teaspoon cayenne pepper
> 8 bamboo skewers, soaked in water for 30 minutes

- Blanch garlic in saucepan of rapidly boiling water for 3 minutes.
- Drain garlic well and set aside.
- In a large bowl stir together oil, tomato sauce, vinegar, basil, salt and cayenne pepper.
- Add shrimp and toss together.
- Refrigerate for about 20 minutes.
- Remove shrimp from marinade (reserving remaining marinade).
- Thread shrimp and garlic alternately on skewers.
- Place skewers on a hot grill, turning once or twice and brushing with reserved marinade.
- Shrimp will be done when it becomes pink, about 6 – 8 minutes.

Tip: When threading shrimp on skewers, bend each shrimp almost in half, so that the large end nearly touches the smaller tail end. Insert the skewer just above the tail, so that it passes through the body twice. And remember that shrimp cooks quickly when grilled!

Shrimp

SOUTHERN FRIED SHRIMP

> 2 pounds large shrimp, peeled and deveined
> 2 large eggs
> 1/4 cup cornstarch
> 1/4 cup yellow cornmeal
> Vegetable oil for frying
> Salt to taste

- In a shallow dish, beat eggs lightly.
- Place cornstarch and cornmeal in separate dishes.
- Dip shrimp in cornstarch, then in egg and then in cornmeal.
- In a large skillet, heat 1/4" oil until very hot (but not smoking).
- Fry shrimp a few at a time (not crowding pan) until cooked through and pink.
- Drain fried shrimp on paper towels.
- Continuing frying shrimp a few at a time until finished with remaining shrimp.
- Serve shrimp immediately.

Tip: Great with salsa on the side (use bottled salsa or see Grilled Mahimahi with Tomato Salsa recipe).

SHRIMP WITH GREEN DIP

> 2 pounds large or jumbo shrimp, peeled and deveined
> Olive oil (about 1/4 cup)
> Salt and pepper to taste

- Toss shrimp with oil until lightly coated.
- Sprinkle with salt and pepper.
- Place shrimp on medium-high grill for 1 1/2 – 2 minutes per side.
- Shrimp may be served warm or cold with chilled dip on the side.

Shrimp

GREEN DIP

---

3 anchovies (2 teaspoons anchovy paste may be substituted)
1/2 cup mayonnaise
1/2 cup sour cream
2 scallions, chopped, both green and white parts
1 cup mixed parsley, basil, thyme and oregano, chopped
1 tablespoon fresh lime juice
1/2 teaspoon salt

- Combine all ingredients in a blender and puree until well blended.
- Serve chilled alongside shrimp.

Tip: The green dip may be prepared up to a day in advance and kept refrigerated until serving.

Weekend Recipes   *(Each Serves 4)*

SHRIMP KEBABS WITH MUSTARD GLAZE

---

2 pounds large shrimp, peeled (but tail shells left on) and deveined
1/4 cup honey
1/4 cup Dijon mustard
2 tablespoons fresh lemon juice
Pinch of dried sage (or oregano)
3 red bell peppers, cut in 2" pieces
3 yellow peppers, cut in 2" pieces
1 small red onion, cut in 1" pieces
8 large mushrooms
8 cherry tomatoes
8 bamboo skewers, soaked in water for 30 minutes

- Combine honey, mustard, lemon juice, and sage (or oregano) in a small dish.
- Alternate shrimp and vegetables on skewers.

Shrimp

- Brush kebabs with honey-mustard glaze and place on medium-high grill.
- Grill kebabs for about 3 minutes.
- Then turn kebabs and grill for another 3 minutes until firm and cooked through.

Tip: These kebabs make up beautifully up to 8 hours ahead of serving. Refrigerate and bring to room temperature before cooking, brush with glaze and grill.

GRILLED SHRIMP WITH PROSCIUTTO AND BASIL

> 2 pounds large shrimp, peeled (but tail shells
>   left on) and deveined
> 1/4 pound paper-thin prosciutto
> 25 – 30 fresh basil leaves
> 1/4 cup fresh lime (or lemon) juice
> 2 tablespoons olive oil
> Pepper to taste
> 10 bamboo skewers, soaked in water for 30 minutes

- Wrap each shrimp in a basil leaf and half slice of prosciutto.
- Slide shrimp onto skewers (sliding skewer tip first through body and then tail), lightly touching each other.
- Whisk together lime juice, oil and pepper in a small dish.
- Brush skewers with lime marinade and marinate for 15 minutes only.
- Place skewers on medium-high grill and cook for about 5 minutes.
- Turn skewers and grill for another 5 minutes until just cooked through.

Note: The lime juice will begin to "cook" the shrimp if marinated for more than 15 minutes. No salt was added because of the salty prosciutto.

Shrimp

MARGARITA SHRIMP

2 pounds medium shrimp, peeled and deveined
4 tablespoons fresh lime juice
Salt and pepper to taste
2 small ripe avocados
2 tablespoons butter, unsalted
2 tablespoons shallots, finely chopped
1/3 cup tequila
1 cup heavy cream (no substitute)
1/4 teaspoon hot pepper flakes
1/4 cup cilantro, chopped

- In a mixing bowl, combine shrimp, 3 tablespoons lime juice, salt and pepper.
- Let shrimp marinate for 15 – 20 minutes.
- Peel and remove pits from avocados and cut into 1/2" slices.
- Dip avocados in remaining lime juice to prevent darkening.
- Melt butter in a large frying pan.
- Add shrimp and marinade, cooking over high heat for 1 minute.
- Add shallots, cooking for about 10 seconds.
- Add tequila, cream, salt, pepper and pepper flakes.
- Stir briefly and then add avocado slices.
- Cook for about another minute.
- Using a slotted spoon, remove shrimp and avocado to a serving dish.
- Bring sauce to a full rolling boil for about 1 minute, then add cilantro.
- Spoon sauce over shrimp and serve.

Shrimp

A DIFFERENT SHRIMP SCAMPI

> 2 pounds large or jumbo shrimp, peeled and deveined
> 1 1/2 tablespoons olive oil
> 2 large cloves garlic, minced
> 1 tablespoon shallots, minced
> 2 tablespoons brandy
> 2 teaspoons fresh lemon juice
> 1 1/2 tablespoons parsley, chopped
> Dash of salt
> 1/4 teaspoon pepper
> 4 tablespoons unsalted butter, softened

- In a large skillet (or wok) heat oil until nearly smoking.
- Add shrimp and cook until just opaque, about 1 minute per side.
- Remove shrimp to plate and hold.
- Add a little more oil to skillet and then add garlic and shallots.
- Cook until just fragrant, do not brown, about 10 seconds.
- Add brandy, lemon juice, parsley, salt and pepper.
- Cook until well reduced, then remove pan from heat and swirl in butter.
- Add shrimp and toss them to coat with sauce.
- Serve sprinkled with chopped parsley.

Shrimp

SHRIMP AND ASPARAGUS FRITTATA

1/4 pound small, cleaned and cooked shrimp
3 small red-skinned potatoes, sliced 1/8" thick
3 tablespoons olive oil
Pinch of salt
1/4 pound fresh asparagus, trimmed and cut into 2" lengths
6 large eggs, at room temperature
2 ounces thinly sliced prosciutto, chopped coarsely
Pepper to taste

- Heat 2 tablespoons oil in a skillet over medium heat.
- Add potatoes and cook until tender and lightly browned.
- Sprinkle with salt and remove pan from heat.
- Steam or boil asparagus until just tender.
- Beat eggs lightly in a bowl.
- Add asparagus, shrimp, prosciutto, pepper and potatoes, stirring to coat evenly.
- Add remaining oil to skillet and return to medium heat.
- Add egg mixture, spreading evenly in skillet.
- Cook until egg has begun to set at edges but is still runny in the middle (about 5 minutes).
- Place skillet under broiler for several minutes to brown top and finish cooking eggs.
- Slide frittata out of the pan onto a platter.
- May be served hot, warm or at room temperature!

Shrimp

BAKED STUFFED SHRIMP

> 2 pounds jumbo shrimp, peeled, deveined and butterflied
>   (see note below)
> 1 tablespoon olive oil
> 3 green onions, minced
> 1 large clove garlic, minced
> 1 tablespoon (total) chopped parsley, thyme, oregano and marjoram
> 2 slices bacon, cooked and finely chopped
> 3/4 cup fresh bread crumbs
> 1 tablespoon grated Parmesan cheese
> Salt and pepper to taste
> Lemon wedges

- Preheat oven to 450°F.
- Heat oil in a skillet on medium heat.
- Add onions, garlic and herbs until onions just soften.
- Remove from heat and put in a bowl.
- Add bacon crumbles, bread crumbs, cheese, salt and pepper.
- Lay shrimp on a lightly oiled baking sheet, cut side down, with tails pointing up.
- Place a layer of stuffing on the flat surface of each shrimp, mounding slightly.
- Bake until shrimp have turned pink and stuffing is nicely browned, 10 – 12 minutes.

Tip: If desired tartar or remoulade sauce may be served. For a special evening, replace bacon with 1/2 pound crabmeat.

Note: To butterfly, cut shrimp down its center lengthwise, but not quite through, leaving both halves attached. The shrimp is then spread to resemble a butterfly.

Tilapia, Snapper and Flounder

This section groups together tilapia, snapper and flounder because any of the three may be used in the following recipes. Each is a moderately firm fish with a mild flavor and prepares well baked, broiled or sautéed. Each of these three fish, however, cooks quickly and often ends up being overcooked (and ruined). To reduce the likelihood of this, simply fold the fillets in half before cooking. Remember to rinse tilapia, snapper and flounder fillets in cold water and then pat dry with paper towels prior to cooking.

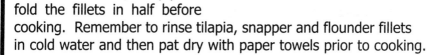

Tilapia

Believed to have originated in the Nile River, tilapia is now farm raised throughout the world. According to biblical legend, Jesus multiplied tilapia to feed the hungry, and St. Peter caught tilapia in the Red Sea, giving it the nickname of "St. Peter's Fish."

Tilapia is low in fat and has a sweet, mild flavor. Its meat is fairly firm, with a light, flaky texture. The whole tilapia is generally 1 – 2 pounds and has white to pinkish meat.

You should buy fresh or frozen tilapia fillets, using fresh fillets within two to three days of purchase.

Nutritional Information

Tilapia	*Serving size: 100g/3.5oz raw*
Calories	85
Fat Calories	9
Total Fat	1g
Saturated Fat	0.4g
Carbohydrates	0.0g
Cholesterol	50mg
Sodium	35mg
Protein	18g
Omega-3	N/A

Snapper

There are many species of snapper, but the most common are red, yellowtail, lane, hognose and gray. Most snapper sold in U.S. supermarkets and wholesale clubs is red snapper, which generally has the best flavor and texture.

Snapper, unlike tilapia, is not farm raised. Red snapper is typically caught in the Gulf of Mexico, but also is found from the Carolinas to Brazil. Although widely available year round, snapper is most plentiful during the summer months.

Although red snapper is fattier than many other types of fish, it is very low in saturated fat and contains the important omega-3s. The whole red snapper is typically 4 – 6 pounds, with a metallic pink to reddish meat. The meat has a great, mild flavor with a fairly firm consistency.

Like tilapia, you should purchase fresh or frozen snapper fillets from your local supermarket or wholesale club and use fresh fillets within two to three days of purchase.

Nutritional Information

Red Snapper	*Serving size: 100g/3.5oz raw*
Calories	110
Fat Calories	24
Total Fat	2.6g
Saturated Fat	0.5g
Carbohydrates	0.0g
Cholesterol	40mg
Sodium	96mg
Protein	20.2g
Omega-3	0.6g

Flounder

Flounder is a large fish, with a flat oval shape, that is caught in both the Atlantic and the Pacific. Flounder, like snapper, is not farm raised. Flounder is quite a versatile fish. It prepares wonderfully with almost any method of cooking and may be combined with a variety of flavors while maintaining its natural taste.

Flounder has a delicate flavor, with firm, finely textured meat. Whole flounder is generally 1 – 5 pounds, with pink or white flesh. Flounder is packed with protein and extremely low in fat and calories.

As with both tilapia and snapper, you should buy fresh or frozen flounder fillets and use fresh fillets within two to three days of purchase.

Nutritional Information

Flounder	Serving size: 100g/3.5oz raw
Calories	91
Fat Calories	10.8
Total Fat	1.2g
Saturated Fat	0.3g
Carbohydrates	0.0g
Cholesterol	48mg
Sodium	81mg
Protein	18.8g
Omega-3	0.2g

Tilapia, Snapper and Flounder

Weeknight Recipes *(Each Serves 4)*

SAUTÉED FILLETS WITH SALSA

1 1/2 – 2 pounds of tilapia, snapper or flounder fillets
1 clove garlic, minced
1/4 cup onion, chopped
1/4 cup celery, chopped
1 tablespoon parsley, chopped
1 tablespoon celery leaves, coarsely chopped
2 teaspoons olive or canola oil
1/2 cup salsa (use bottled or see Grilled Mahimahi
  with Tomato Salsa recipe)

- In a medium sauté pan heat oil to medium high.
- Sauté garlic, onion and celery until just tender.
- Add fillets, parsley and celery leaves.
- Sauté for about 3 minutes, then lower heat to medium.
- Turn fillets and add salsa.
- Continue cooking for another 2 – 3 minutes, until fish flakes easily.
- Serve immediately.

Tip: Remember to fold fillets in half to avoid overcooking.

Tilapia, Snapper and Flounder

BAKED FILLETS IN WHITE WINE

> 1 1/2 – 2 pounds of tilapia, snapper or flounder fillets
> 1 medium onion, thinly sliced
> 1 medium green pepper, thinly sliced
> 1 teaspoon fresh thyme or 1/2 teaspoon dried
> Salt and pepper to taste
> 1 tablespoon olive oil
> 1/3 cup white wine
> 1 medium tomato, chopped
> Lemon wedges

- Preheat oven to 400°F.
- Lightly oil a baking sheet, and then arrange onions and peppers on sheet.
- Place fillets on top of vegetables.
- Sprinkle fillets with thyme, salt and pepper to taste.
- Brush fillets with oil and drizzle wine over the fish.
- Bake for 15 – 20 minutes, until cooked through.
- Sprinkle tomato on top and serve with lemon wedges.

Note: Mrs. Dash makes a great substitution for the thyme.

FILLETS DIJON

> 1 1/2 – 2 pounds of tilapia, snapper or flounder fillets
> 2 tablespoons mayonnaise
> 2 teaspoons Dijon mustard
> 1/2 teaspoon lemon juice
> Salt and pepper to taste
> Lemon wedges

- Preheat oven to 350°F.
- Fold fillets in half and place in a 13 x 9-inch glass baking dish.
- Sprinkle fish with salt and pepper.
- Combine mayo, mustard and lemon juice.
- Spread mayo mixture evenly over fillets.
- Bake uncovered for about 20 minutes, until topping is golden brown and fish flakes easily.
- Serve with lemon wedges.

Tilapia, Snapper and Flounder

BROILED FILLETS WITH OLIVE BUTTER

> 1 1/2 – 2 pounds of tilapia, snapper or flounder fillets
> Olive oil
> Salt and pepper to taste
> 1/4 cup unsalted butter, softened
> 1/8 cup green or black olives, chopped
> 1/8 teaspoon dry mustard

- Lightly brush a baking pan with oil and add fillets in a single layer.
- Combine butter, olives and mustard in a small dish.
- Broil fish on high for about 5 minutes, watching it carefully to avoid overcooking.
- Just before fish is done, spread olive butter on top and continue broiling until butter melts.
- Serve immediately.

BAKED FILLETS WITH HAM AND OLIVE BUTTER

> 1 1/2 – 2 pounds of tilapia, snapper or flounder fillets
> Salt and pepper to taste
> 1/4 cup unsalted butter, softened
> 1/8 cup green or black olives, chopped
> 1/8 teaspoon dry mustard
> 4 slices ham, thinly sliced

- Preheat oven to 350°F.
- Combine butter, olives and mustard in a small dish.
- Lay each fillet on a piece of waxed paper (or plastic wrap).
- Place a ham slice on each fillet and top with a spoonful of butter mixture.
- Roll up fillets and bake for about 15 minutes, until cooked through.
- Baste fillets with drippings.
- Serve immediately.

Tilapia, Snapper and Flounder

BREADED FILLETS WITH HERBS

> 1 1/2 – 2 pounds of tilapia, snapper or flounder fillets
> 1 1/3 cups dry bread crumbs (homemade if you have time)
> 1 teaspoon Herbes de Provence (see note below)
> 2 teaspoons fresh parsley, chopped
> 1/2 teaspoon salt
> 2 eggs
> 1/4 cup heavy cream
> 1/2 cup butter
> Lemon wedges

- In a shallow dish, combine bread crumbs, Herbes de Provence, parsley and salt.
- In another shallow dish, whisk eggs and cream.
- Add fillets to egg mixture, coating both sides and leaving in mixture for 5 minutes.
- Dip each fillet in bread crumbs, coating both sides well.
- Melt 1/2 of butter in a large sauté pan on medium-high heat.
- Add 1/2 of fillets (do not crowd pan) and cook for about 2 minutes.
- Flip fillets and cook for another 2 minutes or so, until just browned and fish flakes easily.
- Remove fillets from pan and repeat with remaining butter and uncooked fillets.
- Serve immediately with fresh lemon wedges.

Note: Herbes de Provence is now found in most supermarkets. It is an aromatic mixture of herbs, reflecting the common mixture of dried herbs used in southern France. The herbs usually included are thyme, bay leaves, rosemary, summer savory, cloves, lavender, tarragon, chervil, sage, marjoram, basil, fennel seed and orange zest.

Tilapia, Snapper and Flounder

Weekend Recipes   *(Each Serves 4)*

BAKED FILLETS WITH PARMESAN GLAZE

> 1 1/2 – 2 pounds of tilapia, snapper or flounder fillets
> 1/3 cup mayonnaise
> 1/2 cup Parmesan
> 1 tablespoon lemon zest
> 1 tablespoon fresh lemon juice
> 1 clove garlic, minced
> 1/2 teaspoon Worcestershire sauce
> 2 tablespoons parsley, chopped

- Preheat broiler to high and place rack 4" below heat.
- Lightly salt and pepper fillets.
- Lay fillets on waxed paper (or plastic wrap) and roll up.
- Whisk mayo, Parmesan, zest, lemon juice, garlic and Worcestershire sauce in a small bowl.
- Spray broiler pan with nonstick cooking spray.
- Place fillets seam side down and broil until tops are lightly browned, about 7 – 8 minutes.
- Remove browned fish and top with mayo mixture.
- Return to broiler and cook for 1 – 2 minutes, until fish is deep golden brown and bubbling.
- Sprinkle parsley on top and serve immediately.

Tilapia, Snapper and Flounder

SAUTÉED FILLETS WITH BLACK OLIVE VINAIGRETTE

> 1 1/2 – 2 pounds of tilapia, snapper or flounder fillets
> 1/3 cup flour
> 1/3 cup Kalamata olives, pitted and coarsely chopped
> 1/3 cup plus 2 tablespoons olive oil
> 1 tablespoon lemon zest
> 1 clove garlic, minced
> 1/8 teaspoon red pepper flakes
> 4 – 5 cups baby arugula, rinsed and dry
> Lemon wedges

- Lightly salt and pepper fillets, then lightly coat with flour.
- Whisk olives, 1/3 cup olive oil, zest, garlic and pepper flakes.
- Add 2 tablespoons olive oil to a sauté pan on medium-high heat.
- Reduce heat to medium and place 2 fillets in pan, cooking for 4 – 5 minutes.
- Flip fish and cook until nicely browned, about 3 more minutes.
- Transfer fillets to a platter and cover to keep warm.
- Repeat with remaining uncooked fillets.
- Toss arugula with olive vinaigrette.
- Place salad on plates and top with fillets, spooning additional vinaigrette on top.
- Serve immediately with lemon wedges.

LEMON-DILL FILLETS

> 1 1/2 – 2 pounds of tilapia, snapper or flounder fillets
> 3 tablespoons butter, unsalted
> 1 tablespoon fresh dill, chopped
> 2 tablespoons fresh lemon juice
> Salt and pepper to taste
> 2 green onions, white and green parts, chopped

- Melt butter in a nonstick skillet on medium heat.
- Add dill, lemon juice, salt and pepper.
- Sauté several minutes, stirring.
- Add fillets and cook for about 10 – 12 minutes, basting with butter until cooked through.
- Serve immediately.

Tilapia, Snapper and Flounder

FILLET EN PAPILLOTE

---
2 (8 ounce) tilapia, snapper or flounder fillets
Parchment paper
Salt and pepper to taste
1/2 cup plus 2 tablespoons butter, divided
1 onion, finely chopped
1 cup flour
2 cups milk, scalded
2 eggs
Dash Tabasco
Dash nutmeg
2 tablespoons white wine
1/2 pound medium shrimp, cooked and chopped

- Preheat oven to 350°F.
- Melt 1/2 cup butter in sauté pan on medium heat.
- Cook onions until tender (about 5 minutes).
- Slowly stir in flour, until a paste is formed.
- When mixture is dry, slowly add scalded milk, stirring constantly until thickened.
- Remove from heat.
- In a small bowl, mix eggs, Tabasco, nutmeg and wine.
- Add mixture and shrimp to sauce in sauté pan.
- Cut parchment paper large enough for fillets with extra length for folding.
- Brush paper with 2 tablespoons melted butter.
- Pour 1/3 sauce mixture onto paper and place 1 fillet on top of sauce.
- Add 1/3 more sauce on top of fillet.
- Place remaining fillet on top, and then cover fillet with remaining sauce.
- Fold parchment over fillets, crimping edges well.
- Bake for 30 minutes.
- Remove from paper and serve immediately with lemon wedges.

Catfish

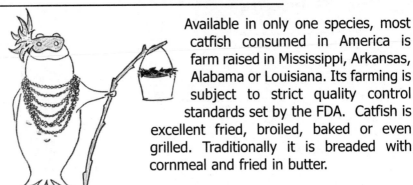

Available in only one species, most catfish consumed in America is farm raised in Mississippi, Arkansas, Alabama or Louisiana. Its farming is subject to strict quality control standards set by the FDA. Catfish is excellent fried, broiled, baked or even grilled. Traditionally it is breaded with cornmeal and fried in butter.

Farm-raised catfish has a mild and sweet flavor, due in part to its controlled diet and environment. A whole catfish averages 1 1/2 pounds, with whitish meat that has no "fishy" odor.

You should buy fresh or frozen catfish fillets from your supermarket or wholesale club and use fresh fillets within two to three days of purchase. Remember to rinse catfish fillets in cold water and then pat dry with paper towels prior to cooking.

Nutritional Information

Catfish	Serving size: 100g/3.5oz raw
Calories	135
Fat Calories	68
Total Fat	7.6g
Saturated Fat	1.8g
Carbohydrates	0.0g
Cholesterol	47mg
Sodium	53mg
Protein	15.5g
Omega-3	0.6g

Catfish

Weeknight Recipes   *(Each Serves 4)*

BROILED CATFISH DIJON

---

4 catfish fillets (6 ounces)
3 tablespoons butter, melted
1 teaspoon Worcestershire sauce
1 teaspoon lemon pepper seasoning
2 teaspoons Dijon mustard

- Preheat broiler to high.
- Mix butter, Worcestershire sauce, lemon pepper and mustard in a small bowl.
- Brush both sides of fillets well with mixture.
- Place fillets on a broiler pan, 6" from heat, cooking for 5 – 6 minutes.
- Flip fillets and cook for another 5 – 6 minutes, until fish flakes easily.

Tip: May also be grilled using heavy duty aluminum foil for same amount of time. If grilled, do not turn fish.

Catfish

CATFISH WITH CORNBREAD STUFFING

4 catfish fillets (6 ounces)
Salt and pepper to taste
2 tablespoons unsalted butter
1 small onion, chopped fine
1/2 cup celery, chopped fine
1 6-ounce package seasoned cornbread stuffing mix
1 1/2 cups water
Lemon wedges

- Melt butter in a medium sauté pan over medium heat.
- Add fillets and cook for 3 – 5 minutes.
- Add onion and celery, and cook for another 3 – 5 minutes, until fish flakes.
- Remove fish from pan, cover to keep warm.
- Add water to the same skillet and bring to a boil.
- Add cornbread stuffing and cover for 5 minutes.
- Serve catfish with stuffing and lemon wedges.

CAJUN CATFISH

4 catfish fillets (6 ounces)
1/2 cup tomato sauce
2 packages (3/4 oz. each) cheese garlic salad dressing mix
1 1/2 tablespoons vegetable oil
2 tablespoons fresh parsley, chopped
2 tablespoons parmesan cheese, grated

- Preheat oven to 350°F.
- In a bowl, combine tomato sauce, dressing, oil and parsley.
- Brush fish with sauce and place in a well greased baking dish.
- Cover fish with remaining sauce and top with cheese.
- Let stand for 20 – 30 minutes.
- Bake fish for about 20 minutes, until flakes easily.
- Turn oven to broil and broil fish 3" from heat for 1 – 2 minutes, until browned and crispy.
- Serve immediately.

Catfish

EASY BAKED CATFISH

4 catfish fillets (6 ounces)
1 teaspoon salt
Dash pepper
1/2 cup green onions, thinly sliced
1 lemon, very thinly sliced
1/2 cup catsup
1 1/2 tablespoons vegetable oil
2 tablespoons white wine

- Preheat oven to 350°F.
- Place fillets in a well greased baking dish.
- Sprinkle fish with salt and pepper.
- Spread onion over fish and top with lemon slices.
- Combine catsup, oil and wine, and pour over fish.
- Bake for 20 – 25 minutes, until flakes easily.
- Serve immediately.

Weekend Recipes   *(Each Serves 4)*

GRILLED SESAME CATFISH

4 catfish fillets (6 ounces)
1/2 cup vegetable or canola oil
1/4 cup sesame seeds
2 tablespoons lemon juice
1/2 teaspoon salt
Pepper to taste
Lemon wedges

- Place fillets in a flat fish basket for the grill.
- Combine remaining ingredients and baste fish.
- Grill fish on medium heat about 4" from heat for about 8 minutes.
- Baste with the sauce and turn.
- Continue grilling for another 7 – 10 minutes, until flakes easily.
- Serve immediately with lemon wedges.

Catfish

CATFISH WITH MUSTARD SAUCE

4 catfish fillets (6 ounces)
Salt and pepper to taste
2 1/2 tablespoons butter, melted
1 teaspoon Worcestershire sauce
1 teaspoon lemon pepper seasoning

- Preheat broiler to high.
- Combine butter, Worcestershire sauce and lemon pepper.
- Brush both sides of fish with mixture.
- Place fish on a broiler pan.
- Broil about 6" from heat for 12 – 15 minutes, until flakes easily.
- Spoon mustard sauce over fillets and serve.

MUSTARD SAUCE

1 teaspoon Worcestershire sauce
1/2 cup sour cream
1 tablespoon Dijon mustard

- Combine Worcestershire sauce, sour cream and mustard in a small saucepan.
- Heat until warm, careful not to boil as sour cream will curdle.
- Spoon over fillets.

Catfish

POACHED CATFISH WITH LEEKS

4 catfish fillets (6 ounces)
1 large leek, sliced
2 shallots, finely chopped
1/2 cup dry white wine
1/2 cup chicken broth
1/4 teaspoon salt
Dash of pepper
1/2 cup heavy cream
2 teaspoons butter
1 tablespoon Dijon mustard
1/2 teaspoon fresh lemon juice

- Rinse leeks well to remove any sand between leaves.
- In small pan, boil leeks in water for 1 minute.
- Plunge leeks into ice water (to stop the cooking), then drain well.
- Place shallots in a skillet that has been well coated with butter.
- Put fillets on top of shallots, then add wine, chicken broth, salt and pepper.
- Add leeks around fish, then cover skillet with buttered parchment paper.
- Bring to a boil, reduce heat and simmer for 12 – 14 minutes, until flakes easily.
- Remove fillets from skillet and keep warm.
- Strain liquids from skillet into a bowl, reserving leeks.
- Return liquid to skillet and bring to a boil.
- Reduce heat and simmer for 2 minutes, uncovered, until reduced to 3/4 cup.
- Add cream and bring to a boil again.
- Reduce heat and simmer for 2 minutes, until sauce begins to thicken and is reduced by half.
- Whisk in butter, mustard and lemon juice.
- Add reserved leeks and cook 1 minute, until hot.
- Spoon sauce over fillets and serve.

Tuna and Swordfish

This section groups together tuna and swordfish because either may be used in the following recipes. Each is a firm fish with excellent flavor and prepares well baked, broiled, sautéed or grilled (although grilling often produces the best results). Like salmon, both tuna and swordfish marinate very well, and may remain in a marinade for up to 6 hours. Remember to rinse tuna and swordfish steaks in cold water and then pat dry with paper towels prior to cooking.

Tuna and Swordfish
Tuna

Although most Americans have eaten canned tuna fish, many are just beginning to enjoy the wonderful taste of tuna steaks. Tuna is a member of the mackerel family and comes in a number of species, including yellowfin, bluefin and albacore. Yellowfin is the most common tuna that is sold in supermarkets and wholesale clubs.

Tuna is not farm raised. It is caught in deep, warm waters of both the Atlantic and the Pacific. Tuna are fast swimmers and migrate across large distances.

Tuna has a distinct, delicious flavor, with a dense texture. The whole tuna ranges from 40 – 80 pounds, with reddish meat. It is an extremely healthful choice, low in fat and rich in protein and omega-3s.

You should buy fresh or frozen tuna steaks from your local supermarket or wholesale club, and like most other fish, use fresh steaks within two to three days of purchase. Tuna is one of the best fish for leftovers, as it can be readily used in salads and spreads.

Nutritional Information

Tuna	Serving size: 100g/3.5oz raw
Calories	108
Fat Calories	8.1
Total Fat	0.9g
Saturated Fat	0.2g
Carbohydrates	0.0g
Cholesterol	45mg
Sodium	37mg
Protein	23.4g
Omega-3	0.6g

Tuna and Swordfish
Swordfish

With its great taste and texture, swordfish is now one of the most popular fish in America. As its name suggests, it has a long, blade-like nose. Not farm raised, swordfish is caught in ocean waters all over the world, typically at night during a bright moon (when the swordfish itself prefers to feed).

Available in only one species, swordfish is loaded with protein and is relatively low in saturated fat. It also contains the healthful omega-3s. Despite initial concerns about mercury, studies have shown swordfish to be quite safe when eaten in moderation. (People in "high risk" categories, such as very young children and pregnant or nursing mothers should, of course, limit their mercury intake based upon their physician's advice.)

Swordfish has a meaty flavor that tastes somewhat like high-quality beef. Its flesh ranges from pinkish white to orange. The whole swordfish is very large, averaging 50 – 200 pounds. A swordfish steak has whorls (resembling the cross section of a tree).

As always, buy fresh or frozen swordfish steaks at your local supermarket or wholesale club and prepare fresh steaks within two to three days of purchase.

Nutritional Information

Swordfish	*Serving size: 100g/3.5oz raw*
Calories	121
Fat Calories	36
Total Fat	4.0g
Saturated Fat	1.1g
Carbohydrates	0.0g
Cholesterol	39mg
Sodium	90mg
Protein	19.8g
Omega-3	0.9g

Tuna and Swordfish

Weeknight Recipes   *(Each Serves 4)*

PAN BLACKENED STEAKS

> 4 tuna or swordfish steaks (1 1/2 – 2 pounds total)
> 2 teaspoons garlic powder
> 1 teaspoon onion powder
> 2 tablespoons Italian herbs
> 1 teaspoon dry parsley
> 2 teaspoons olive oil
> Lemon wedges

- Combine garlic powder, onion powder, Italian herbs and parsley.
- Rub mixture on both sides of steaks.
- Heat oil in a large skillet to medium high.
- Cook steaks about 3 minutes.
- Flip steaks and cook for about another 3 minutes, until flakes easily.
- Serve immediately with lemon wedges.

GRILLED DIJON STEAKS

> 4 tuna or swordfish steaks (1 1/2 – 2 pounds total)
> 1/2 cup mayonnaise
> 2 1/2 tablespoons Dijon mustard
> 2 teaspoons fresh lemon juice
> 2 dashes Tabasco
> Salt and pepper to taste
> Lemon wedges

- Preheat grill to medium high.
- In small bowl, mix mayo, mustard, lemon juice, Tabasco, salt and pepper.
- Spread sauce on both sides of fish, coating well.
- Grill for about 5 minutes.
- Carefully turn, then grill for another 5 minutes, until flakes easily.
- Serve immediately with lemon wedges.

Note: Steaks can be coated with sauce and refrigerated for up to 8 hours before cooking. Steaks may also be broiled (instead of grilled) for similar cooking times.

Tuna and Swordfish

Weekend Recipes *(Each Serves 4)*

GRILLED STEAKS PROVENÇAL

> 4 tuna or swordfish steaks (1 1/2 – 2 pounds total)
> Salt and pepper to taste
> 1 tablespoon fresh ginger root, grated
> 1 tablespoon fresh lemon juice
> 1 tablespoon olive oil

- Sprinkle both sides of steaks with salt, pepper and ginger root.
- Rub steaks with lemon juice and oil.
- Heat grill to medium high and grill steaks 5 minutes on each side, until flakes easily.
- Top steaks with sauce and serve.

PROVENÇAL SAUCE

> 1 ripe tomato
> 1/4 cup olive oil
> 2 tablespoons red wine vinegar
> 1/4 cup shallots, finely chopped
> 1 teaspoon garlic, finely minced
> 1/4 cup fresh basil, chopped
> 1/2 teaspoon grated lemon rind
> Pepper to taste

- Blanch tomato in boiling water for 8 seconds, then remove and drain.
- When cool enough to handle, remove tomato skin.
- Cut tomato in half and remove seeds, then cut into cubes.
- Add oil, vinegar, shallots, garlic, basil, lemon rind and pepper.
- Blend well, then spoon over steaks.

Tuna and Swordfish

GRILLED SANGRIA STEAKS

> 4 tuna or swordfish steaks (1 1/2 – 2 pounds total)
> 4 tablespoons butter, chilled, cut into 4 pieces
> Lemon wedges

- After marinating steaks (see sangria directions below), preheat grill to medium high.
- Grill steaks about 5 minutes on each side, until flakes easily.
- While grilling, bring reserved sangria to a boil.
- Remove sangria from heat and whisk in butter, one piece at a time, until well blended.
- Top grilled steaks with sangria and serve with lemon wedges.

SANGRIA SAUCE AND MARINADE

> Salt and pepper to taste
> 3 cups Beaujolais or Merlot
> 1/3 cup sugar
> 1 lemon, sliced thin
> 1 lime, sliced thin
> 2 whole cloves
> 1 tablespoon vanilla
> 1/4 cup canola or vegetable oil

- In a saucepan, boil wine, sugar, lemon, lime and cloves, until reduced to 1 cup.
- Strain mixture, discarding solids.
- Stir in vanilla and chill.
- Reserve 1/4 cup of sangria for sauce (see above).
- Whisk oil into remaining sangria for marinade.
- Rinse steaks and pat dry with paper towels, then marinate for 2 – 6 hours.

Tuna and Swordfish

BROILED STEAKS WITH GINGER SAUCE

4 tuna or swordfish steaks (1 1/2 – 2 pounds total)
Salt and pepper to taste
2 tablespoons unsalted butter, melted
1 tablespoon Dijon mustard
2 tablespoons mayonnaise

- Preheat broiler to high heat.
- Sprinkle steaks with salt and pepper.
- Brush both sides of steaks with butter.
- Combine mustard and mayo, then spread on both sides of steaks.
- Broil steaks about 5" from heat for about 4 – 5 minutes.
- Carefully turn steaks and broil for another 5 minutes, until flakes easily.
- Top steaks with ginger sauce (either warm or room temperature).
- Serve immediately.

GINGER SAUCE

3 tablespoons ground ginger
1 tablespoon garlic, finely minced
3 tablespoons light soy sauce
3/4 cup water
4 tablespoons olive oil
2 tablespoons fresh cilantro leaves
Pepper to taste

- In a small saucepan, combine ginger, garlic, soy sauce, water and oil.
- Bring to a boil over medium heat.
- Reduce heat and simmer for about 15 minutes, whisking occasionally.
- Remove from heat, and stir in cilantro and pepper.
- Spoon on top of broiled steaks.

Cod

People often compare other fish to cod –
"it's like cod, but a bit fishier" or "it
tastes like cod, but has denser meat." Cod is
from the same family of fish that includes
haddock and pollock. It is not farm
raised. Atlantic cod, as its name
suggests, is harvested from the
depths of the North Atlantic. There
is also Pacific cod, but the two
species are almost indistinguishable after being filleted. "Scrod" is
simply cod that is under 2 1/2 pounds – it is not a separate species
of fish.

Cod is rich in protein, extremely low in fat and also has omega-3s.
It has a mild flavor that makes it a terrific "base" for other flavors.
Many people who do not care for "fishy" seafood love cod because
of its neutral taste.

Whole cod ranges from 2 – 25 pounds, with white to pinkish meat
that turns to an opaque white when cooked. You should buy fresh
or frozen cod from your local supermarket or wholesale club
and prepare fresh fillets within two to three days of purchase.
Remember to rinse cod fillets in cold water and then pat dry with
paper towels prior to cooking.

Nutritional Information

Cod	Serving size: 100g/3.5oz raw
Calories	82
Fat Calories	6.3
Total Fat	0.7g
Saturated Fat	0.1g
Carbohydrates	0.0g
Cholesterol	43mg
Sodium	54mg
Protein	17.8g
Omega-3	0.2g

Cod

Weeknight Recipes

BROILED COD

---

4 cod fillets (about 2 pounds total)
2 tablespoons vegetable oil
2 – 3 tablespoons seasoned cracker crumbs
Pepper to taste
Butter pieces to dot on fish
Lemon wedges

- Preheat broiler to high.
- Generously coat both sides of fillets with oil.
- Place fillets in a broiler pan, then pepper.
- Broil fillets 3 – 4″ below heat for about 8 minutes.
- Top fillets with cracker crumbs and butter pieces.
- Continue broiling until lightly browned and flakes easily.
- Serve immediately with lemon wedges.

BAKED COD PARMIGIANA

---

4 cod fillets (about 2 pounds total)
1/2 cup olive oil
1 1/2 cups tomato sauce
1 large onion, thinly sliced
1 green pepper, thinly sliced
1 jalapeno, minced (optional)
1 garlic clove, minced
1 cup mushrooms, sliced
1 tablespoon fresh basil, chopped
4 ounces mozzarella cheese, grated
1/2 cup Parmesan cheese, grated

Cod

- Preheat oven to 400°F.
- In a large skillet, heat 1/4 cup oil to medium high.
- Brown fillets quickly on both sides.
- In bottom of baking dish, place 1/2 cup tomato sauce, then top with fillets.
- In skillet, add 1/4 cup oil.
- Sauté onion, green pepper, jalapeno and garlic for about 2 minutes, stirring frequently.
- Stir in mushrooms, basil and remaining tomato sauce, simmering for 5 minutes.
- Pour mixture over fillets and sprinkle with cheeses.
- Bake for about 15 minutes, until flakes easily.
- Serve immediately.

SAUTÉED COD WITH OLIVES AND TOMATO

4 cod fillets (about 2 pounds total)
1/4 cup olive oil
4 plum tomatoes, chopped
6 – 8 ripe olives, sliced
Dash dried thyme
4 teaspoons olive oil
2 fresh basil leaves, chopped (or 1 teaspoon dried)

- Heat 1/4 cup oil in heavy sauté pan to medium-high heat.
- Add fillets and cook for 1 minute on each side.
- Add tomatoes, olives and thyme.
- Reduce heat, cover and cook for about 2 minutes.
- Drizzle with remaining olive oil and basil.
- Cover and cook for 2 – 3 more minutes, until flakes easily.
- Serve immediately.

Cod

Weekend Recipes   *(Each Serves 4)*

BAKED COD WITH SHERRY VINAIGRETTE

> 4 cod fillets (about 2 pounds total)
> 1/4 cup sherry vinegar
> 2 teaspoons anchovy paste (or 2 anchovy fillets, minced)
> Salt and pepper to taste
> 1/2 cup olive oil
> 2/3 cup pitted black olives, finely chopped
> 2 teaspoons capers, drained well, finely chopped
> 1 shallot, minced
> 1 garlic clove, minced
> 2 teaspoons fresh oregano (or 1 teaspoon dried)

- Preheat oven to 400°F.
- In small bowl, combine vinegar and anchovy.
- Whisk in salt, pepper, oil, olives, capers, shallot, garlic and oregano, until well mixed.
- Place fillets in large baking dish in one layer.
- Season fillets with pepper.
- Spoon a small amount of vinaigrette over each fillet.
- Drizzle remaining vinaigrette around bottom of baking dish.
- Bake covered with foil for about 25 – 30 minutes, until opaque and firm to the touch.
- Top fillets with pan juices and serve.

Cod

COD WITH FENNEL

---

4 cod fillets (about 2 pounds total)
1 large fennel bulb, thinly sliced (see note below)
1 medium sweet onion, peeled and thinly sliced
2 tablespoons olive oil
Salt and pepper to taste
1 large russet potato, peeled and thinly sliced
1 cup white wine
1 cup chicken stock (canned is fine)
1/4 cup flat-leaf parsley, chopped

- Preheat oven to 425°F.
- Rinse fillets and pat dry with paper towels.
- Heat oil in a large skillet to medium-high heat.
- Sauté fennel and onion for 5 minutes, stirring constantly.
- Add wine and cook until reduced by half.
- Add potatoes to skillet in even layers, completely covering onion and fennel.
- Pour chicken stock evenly around skillet pan.
- Arrange fillets on potatoes, then salt and pepper.
- Bring liquids to a gentle simmer.
- Cover skillet and transfer to oven for about 15 minutes.
- Uncover and continue baking for 3 – 4 minutes, until opaque throughout.
- Serve with parsley, spooning juices over fillets.

Note: To prepare fennel bulb, first trim off tops. Then quarter the bulb and cut each quarter on an angle to remove the core. Finally, cut fennel into thin slices.

Tip: Serve this dish with crusty bread to dip in the juices.

Halibut

Halibut is a mild, white fish that is typically caught in the Pacific waters off the Alaskan coast. It is not farm raised. Halibut has gained popularity in America in recent years largely because of its mild yet meaty flavor and its versatility. In fact, halibut prepares well baked, grilled, broiled, steamed, sautéed or poached.

Halibut, like most other types of fish, is very healthful, with 20 grams of protein and only 0.4 grams of saturated fat per 100 gram serving. It is also one of the best sources of omega-3s.

As mentioned, halibut has a mild, slightly sweet flavor, with dense, white meat. The whole halibut (which like flounder is a flat fish) is quite large, ranging from 10 to over 200 pounds.

You should buy fresh or frozen halibut steaks from your supermarket or wholesale club and use fresh steaks within two to three days of purchase. And remember to rinse halibut steaks in cold water and then pat dry with paper towels prior to cooking.

Nutritional Information

Halibut	*Serving size: 100g/3.5oz raw*
Calories	105
Fat Calories	20
Total Fat	2.2g
Saturated Fat	0.4g
Carbohydrates	0.0g
Cholesterol	32mg
Sodium	63mg
Protein	20g
Omega-3	0.5g

Halibut

BROILED HALIBUT WITH DILL

> 4 halibut fillets (about 1 – 2 pounds total, 1 – 1 1/2" thick)
> 1 tablespoon olive oil
> Salt and pepper to taste

- Preheat broiler to high.
- Brush fillets with oil.
- Salt and pepper fillets and place on a broiler pan.
- Broil about 4" from heat element for 10 – 12 minutes.
- Turn fillets and cook for another 5 – 6 minutes, until flakes easily.
- Spoon dill sauce over fillets and serve immediately.

DILL SAUCE

> 2 tablespoons fresh dill
> 1 tablespoon olive oil
> 2 cups cherry or grape tomatoes, halved
> 1/2 cup sliced green onions

- In a medium skillet, sauté green onions in oil until tender.
- Add tomatoes and dill, cooking until tomatoes are just soft.
- Spoon over halibut fillets.

Halibut

GRILLED HALIBUT

---

4 halibut fillets (about 1 – 2 pounds total, 1 – 1 1/2" thick)
2 tablespoons vegetable oil
Cayenne pepper to taste
Pepper to taste
2 tablespoons butter

- Preheat grill to medium-high heat.
- Season fillets with oil, cayenne pepper and pepper.
- Let fillets marinate for 10 minutes, while grill preheats.
- Sear fillets on both sides.
- Continue grilling for about 10 minutes, until flakes easily.
- Serve with butter dotted on top.

Tip: Sear your fish on the hottest part of the grill and then move to a cooler spot to finish cooking.

Weekend Recipes   *(Each Serves 4)*

GRILLED HALIBUT PACKETS WITH TARRAGON

---

4 halibut fillets (about 1 – 2 pounds total, 1 – 1 1/2" thick)
1/4 cup olive oil
2 medium tomatoes, cut into 8 wedges
1 large fennel bulb, thinly sliced (see note at Cod with Fennel
    recipe)
4 teaspoons fresh tarragon
4 teaspoons lemon zest, grated
8 teaspoons dry vermouth

- Preheat grill to medium-high heat.
- Cut four 12" squares of aluminum foil.
- Place one fillet in each square.
- Drizzle fillets with about 2 teaspoons olive oil, coating both sides.
- Sprinkle with salt and pepper as desired.
- Spread 2 teaspoons olive tapenade on each fillet.

Halibut

- Top each fillet with 2 tomato wedges, 1/4 of fennel, 1 teaspoon zest, 1 teaspoon tarragon and 2 teaspoons vermouth.
- Fold and seal edges very tightly.
- Grill packets with lid closed for about 8 – 9 minutes, until flakes easily.
- Open packets on plates and serve immediately.

OLIVE TAPENADE

1/4 cup black olives, finely chopped
2 teaspoons olive oil
1 clove garlic, crushed
1/2 teaspoon lemon zest

- Combine olives, oil, garlic and lemon zest.

Note: Olive tapenade may be purchased in the specialty food section of most supermarkets.

STEAMED HALIBUT WITH WHITE WINE SAUCE

4 halibut fillets (about 1 – 2 pounds total, 1 – 1 1/2" thick)
1 cup cilantro, chopped
Salt and pepper to taste

- Sprinkle fillets with salt, pepper and cilantro.
- Place fillets in a single layer in steamer basket.
- Steam for about 5 minutes, until flakes easily.
- Spoon sauce over fillets and serve immediately.

Halibut

WHITE WINE SAUCE

```
3/4 cup dry white wine
5 tablespoons butter, unsalted
1 cup mushrooms, sliced with stems
1/3 cup shallots, thinly sliced
2 cups fish broth (or clam juice)
3 tablespoons flour
1 1/2 cups heavy cream
1/4 cup lemon juice
Pepper to taste
```

- In medium saucepan, melt 1 tablespoon butter.
- Add mushrooms and shallots, and sauté on medium heat for about 1 minute.
- Add wine, 1/2 cup fish broth and pepper.
- Simmer until reduced by half.
- In another saucepan, melt 3 tablespoons of butter until bubbly.
- Whisk in flour and then remaining fish broth.
- Simmer for about 10 minutes, stirring well, then add to wine and mushroom sauce.
- Add cream and simmer for about 15 minutes, until nicely thickened.
- Strain through a fine wire strainer and return to pan.
- Stir in lemon juice and then swirl in remaining 1 tablespoon butter.
- Serve very hot over steamed fillets.

Mahimahi

Mahimahi, which is a Hawaiian word, is also known as "mahi-mahi," "dolphin" or "dolphinfish," but it is not related to the marine mammal. It is a single species of fish! And although it is thought of as a Hawaiian fish, mahimahi is actually caught in warm waters throughout the world, including the waters of the Caribbean, Florida, Hawaii and Southern California. It is not farm raised.

Mahimahi is a very nutritious fish, extremely low in calories and fat (with only 0.3 grams of saturated fat per 3 1/2 ounce serving). It is also packed with protein.

Mahimahi has a mild, slightly sweet flavor, with a firm, flaky texture. Its meat generally should be light beige to pinkish in color. Mahimahi is best prepared either on the grill or sautéed.

The whole fish has gorgeous yellow, green and blue colors, and it averages around 5 pounds. You should purchase fresh or frozen mahimahi, and use fresh fillets within two to three days of purchase. As always, remember to rinse mahimahi fillets in cold water and then pat dry with paper towels prior to cooking.

Mahimahi

Nutritional Information

Mahimahi	Serving size: 100g/3.5oz raw
Calories	89
Fat Calories	8
Total Fat	0.9g
Saturated Fat	0.3g
Carbohydrates	0.0g
Cholesterol	86mg
Sodium	128mg
Protein	18.9g
Omega-3	N/A

Weeknight Recipes   *(Each Serves 4)*

GRILLED MAHIMAHI WITH SOY SAUCE

> 4 mahimahi fillets (about 6 – 8 ounces each, 1" thick)
> Salt and pepper to taste
> 2 limes, juiced
> 3 tablespoons dark soy sauce
> 1 1/2 tablespoons ginger root, about a 2" piece
> 1 tablespoon canola or vegetable oil
> Chopped chives (about 20)

- Preheat grill to medium high.
- Lightly salt and pepper fillets.
- In a small bowl, whisk together lime juice, soy sauce, ginger root and oil.
- Place fillets in a shallow glass dish and cover with soy marinade.
- Allow fillets to marinate for about 10 minutes.
- Grill fillets for about 6 minutes on each side, until firm and opaque throughout.
- Garnish with chives and serve immediately.

Tip: If pressed for time, try a bottled soy ginger marinade.

Mahimahi

GRILLED MAHIMAHI WITH TOMATO SALSA

> 4 mahimahi fillets (about 6 – 8 ounces each, 1" thick)
> 1 tablespoon olive oil

- Preheat grill to medium high.
- Brush fillets with oil.
- Grill fillets for about 6 minutes on each side, until firm and opaque throughout.
- Spoon salsa over fillets and serve immediately.

TOMATO SALSA

> 2 medium tomatoes, chopped
> 1/4 cup sweet onion, chopped
> 1 tablespoon olive oil
> 1 garlic clove, minced
> 1/2 teaspoon pepper sauce (Tabasco brand)
> Salt and pepper to taste

- Combine tomatoes, onion, oil, garlic and pepper sauce.
- Add salt and pepper to taste.
- Spoon over fillets.

Tip: To save time, use a bottled salsa or prepare salsa early and refrigerate until needed.

Mahimahi

SAUTÉED MAHIMAHI WITH ALMOND CRABMEAT

> 4 mahimahi fillets (about 6 – 8 ounces each, 1″ thick)
> Flour to dust
> 2 tablespoons butter
> 2 tablespoons fresh lemon juice
> 1/2 bunch green onions

- Dust fillets with flour.
- In a large skillet, melt butter over medium-high heat.
- Add lemon juice.
- Sauté fillets until golden brown on both sides, about 7 1/2 minutes per side.
- Spoon topping over fillets.
- Garnish with green onions and serve immediately.

ALMOND CRABMEAT TOPPING

> 1 onion, finely chopped
> 1/2 cup celery, chopped
> 1 1/2 sticks butter, unsalted
> 1/2 cup parsley, chopped
> 1 1/2 bunches green onions
> 1 pound backfin crabmeat
> 1 cup almond slices, toasted
> 2 tablespoons fresh lemon juice

- In a large saucepan, melt butter over medium heat.
- Sauté onion and celery until tender (but not brown).
- Add parsley and green onions.
- Add crabmeat and almonds, and then heat through.
- Spoon over fillets.

Mahimahi

GRILLED MAHIMAHI WITH CHILE PINEAPPLE SAUCE

4 mahimahi fillets (about 6 – 8 ounces each, 1" thick)
2 cloves garlic, finely chopped
1 tablespoon vegetable oil
Dash of salt

- Preheat grill to medium high.
- Brush fish with oil.
- Season lightly with salt.
- Grill fillets for about 6 minutes on each side, until firm and opaque throughout.
- Spoon sauce over fillets and serve immediately.

CHILE PINEAPPLE SAUCE

1/4 cup shallots, very thinly sliced
1 tablespoon vegetable oil
1 Serrano chile, minced with seeds
1/2 pineapple, peeled, cored and cubed
1 tablespoon Asian fish sauce
1/2 teaspoon sugar
1/3 cup cilantro, chopped

- In medium pan, sauté garlic and shallots in oil on medium heat until soft, about 4 – 5 minutes.
- Add chile and pineapple, cooking for another 5 minutes over medium-high heat.
- Add fish sauce and sugar, and cook for another 30 seconds.
- Remove pan and cool to room temperature.
- Add cilantro and spoon over fillets.

Note: Asian fish sauce is available in the Asian section of your supermarket.

Tip: Pineapple sauce may be prepared ahead of time (without cilantro) and kept refrigerated. Bring to room temperature and add cilantro before serving.

Index

Index

For comments, questions or other correspondence
to the authors, please visit our website at
www.seafoodsimple.com